D1528867

# Kudos for Susan Beth Furst's
## *The Poodle Wears a Pink Tutu*

The Poodle Wears a Pink Tutu may be Susan Beth Furst's first book, but it has all the earmarks of a master poet in the making. She has a strong command of contemporary English language haiku and tanka, inviting the reader into wide-ranging worlds of whimsy, nostalgia, stark reality, transcendence, and redemption where darkness and light flicker and glitter. The poetic landscape is at once hilarious, poignant, startling, and heartwarming.

Make sure you are strapped in and prepare to be enchanted.

**Robert Epstein**
co-author with Ed Markowski of *Memo to Warhol: A Collaboration of Art & Haiku in Color.*

Susan Beth Furst weaves a refreshing journey through her childhood filled with Paddington Bears, the Wizard of Oz, and caramel popcorn. Her travels are chronicled through the various stages, the magical yet honest images evoking joy, disappointment, sadness, and acceptance, all of which add up to one word—life. Through all of this shines Susan's capacity to see the light, to find hope. A recommended book!

High Noon
a glint of sun
on the crossbeam

**Geethanjali Rajan**
author of *longing for sun longing for rain: haiku, senryu, haibun, & tanka prose*

Susan Beth Furst's quirky collection of haiku and tanka is an ingenious mix of simplicity and complexity that leaves a lingering impact.

**Corine Timmer**
award-winning haiku poet and creator of the zodiac haiku anthologies

# The Poodle Wears a Pink Tutu

## Susan Beth Furst

To my mini me

xo
Mom

Jesus
Loves
you

Velvet Dusk Publishing

Cover image by d.Perry
Instagram @d.perryartist

First published in 2024 by Velvet Dusk Publishing
Sacramento, CA

ISBN: 9798877777118

*To Pap,*
*I can still see you grinning from ear to ear,*
*like an old Cheshire cat . . .*

# Contents

# Foreword

I've known Susan Beth Furst, an award-winning haiku poet and Children's Picture Book author, since the Summer of 2017. We are both creative chameleons. Sometimes, it's difficult to keep track of how far we've exchanged communications and book projects, though it's always been an amazing journey.

Susan has published innumerable haiku books of one kind or another for adults, families, and children to lose themselves, as only good books can do! As Susan says, a picture book, which she is famous for doing, is for all ages, as I know only too well. We are both keen on pushing boundaries with haiku and how it's presented as a medium, and 2024, as it unfolds, will be full of further surprises to come!

Although we have never actually met in person, we oddly have Washington DC, America's capital city, to thank for bringing us together, as Susan had been searching for haiku poetry workshops and saw us advertised in a Haiku Society of America newsletter! Since that very first email, we've been to so many different places virtually that we've never jointly lived in or visited. But we have created a creative bond, nevertheless.

Our recent "visit" together wasn't a place (town or city) but a time zone in the 1950s where Narnia was more than just a wardrobe. The collection, *The Poodle Wears a Pink Tutu*, is not only a haiku wonderland of duets, monologues, and triple lines avoiding tripping over each other, but also an extra gift of the classic tanka poetry. It's a veritable *Julefrokost* (Danish: "Christmas meal that lasts an entire day"). The collection goes beyond times past and childhoods and brings contemporary themes, all wrapped up as a grandson sets the course for the Milky Way.

**Alan Summers**
founder, Call of the Page
founder, *Pan Haiku Review*

"My! People come and go so quickly here!"

—*Dorothy, The Wizard of Oz*

The Poodle Wears a Pink Tutu

A Spoonful of Sugar

a lump
under the covers
Paddington Bear
sixty-eight years and
we're still friends

morning whistle
the kettle
up before dawn

slow day . . .
the caramel corn man
pops up a storm

lilypond we dip our toes in the clouds

at the station
belching steam clouds
a row of Pufferbellies

trick or treat
the littlest ghost
wags his tail

clear day
the smokestacks
on strike

a March wind
tugs at the strings
paper tigers

Christmas Eve
a shush of snow
down the chimney

black fishtail gown
Barbie and me
dress for the party

streetlight
I find my way back
to Narnia

Up on the Roof

Tar moon
the way you used
to kiss me
that hot summer
in the city

lemon drops
the candy girl puckers up

sugar plum dreams . . .
the Santa Fe Special
thunders through Plasticville

Bonfire
the s'mores
in your kiss

prom
night
a rustle
in the
pumpkin
patch

protest
the ubiquitous smell
of cannabis

food truck
the sound of reggae
rounds the corner

horsehead nebula
my father says
I can be anything

Venus Diner
we get the munchies
half-way to Mars

Harper's Attic
jazz spilling
into the square

the mummy unwinds Halloween moon

Society's Child

at the home
for unwed mothers
the nurse's aides
wear starched white uniforms
and rock the babies to sleep

dandelions . . .
the neighbourhood
abuzz with the news

afternoon game
the man in the suit
playing hooky

she dreams of flying
no barbed wire
at night

army jacket
I attend my first
peace rally

appalachia the snow men full of coal dust

hypothermia shelter  the surplus population

cobalt blue bottle
her evening
in Paris

Miss America photos
stare at the backs of boozy old men
sitting at the bar

dog days
Grandma sugars up
the blackberries

rabbit
hole
I fall
into
a new
year

MacArthur Park

autumn rain
after the hospital
a trip to the coffee shop
pumpkin spice latte
and your diagnosis

holy
this niggling spot
in my sweater

Elvis takes another spin
blue Christmas

the rustle
of old satin and tulle
gardenias

windblown forsythia
the long and short
of it

the overripe strawberries half-price carpe diem

changing my mind split rock

rainy day
the purples and pinks
of African violets

foggy day
the Alzheimer's unit
playing Sinatra

*Louie, Louie,* still trying to figure out the words

fentanyl
the
slow
drip
of
a
lollipop

Amazing Grace

that book
in the gift shop
and the black beaded bag
how did you know I would need them
for your funeral

Lenten Moon a CAcOPhoNy of bells

silent night
a doe nudges
the fresh fallen snow

Tea party
the Royal Doulton you saved
for a special occasion

all night diner
a sliver of moon
for breakfast

Obit ary my typewriter missing a key

funeral salad
the southern comfort
of lime Jello

Yard Sale
my mother's life
on the front lawn

Anniversary
Dad's irises bloom profusely
this year

High Noon
a glint of sun
on the crossbeam

empty
bucket
all the Easter lilies
flower
the
cross

I Think We're Alone Now

after dark
the fireflies
and us
dancing to the music
of cicadas

French film
we kiss
in black and white

milky way
the transcontinental
clickety-clack

tiptoeing through the tulips
ukulele moon

sweeping up the morning after stardust

cherry blossom
the moon
playing second fiddle

midnight train
to Vermont
*

           *


    *

all that snow

Orient Express a jangle of silver in the galley

orange-pink sunrise
the sidewalk artist
sets up shop

sunday drive so many cows along for the ride

blossom gazing
the poodle wears
a pink tutu

Over the Rainbow

lipstick
on your collar
and you tell me
the moon is made
of green cheese

Oz
the child star pops
another pill

souvenir shop
my sisters and me
choose the Zulu spears

social media even there I wear a mask

pandemic a crack in the snow globe

starry night Wittenberg missing a tree

pied piper even the blind mice smell the coffee

flamingos in Santa hats climate change

in the secret garden
where I left it . . .
my red cape

street fair
the truckers breach
the bouncy castle

Christmas morning
my grandson sets course
for the milky way

# Publication Credits

## Journals

*Blithe Spirit: journal of the British Haiku Society*
*Bloō Outlier Journal*
*Bottle Rockets*
*Cattails*
*Cicada's Cry*
*Contemporary Haibun Online*
*David Labkovski Project, Yom HaShoah Holocaust Commemoration Journal*, 2020
*Failed Haiku*
*Frogpond Journal: Haiku Society of America*
*The Haiku Foundation: Haiku Dialogue*
*haikuKATHA*
*Haikuniverse*
*Hedgerow*
*Human/Kind Journal*

*Mayfly*
*Moonbathing*
*The Pan Haiku Review*
*Presence Haiku Journal*
*Sonic Boom*

## Anthologies

*Dwarf Stars Anthology*, 2019, ed. John C. Mannone

*Hope is a Group Project, a poetry anthology,* ed. Claire Thom, 2022

*Last Train Home: an anthology of contemporary haiku, tanka, and rengay,* ed. Jacqueline Pearce, 2021

*Rip-Roaring Haiku, an anthology of tiger haiku,* ed. Corine Timmer, 2022

*Root, the British Haiku Society members' anthology,* 2019

*They Gave Us Life Celebrating Mothers, Fathers, & Others in Haiku,* ed. Robert Epstein, 2017

*Water, the British Haiku Society members' anthology*, 2022

*Wild Voices: an anthology of short poetry & art by women, Volume 2,* ed. Caroline Skanne, 2018

## Children's Picture Books

*The Amazing Glass House: A Haiku Storybook* by Susan Beth Furst, Purple Cotton Candy Arts, 2019

*Will You Still Love Me?: A Puppy Haiku Story* by Christine L. Villa, Purple Cotton Candy Arts, 2020

# Haiku Poetry Books

*Souvenir Shop* by Susan Beth Furst, Buddha Baby Press, 2018

*Neon Snow* by Susan Beth Furst, Paper Whistle Press, 2019

# Features

"the rustle," selected for the Triveni Haikai India
Spotlight (June 2022)
Host, Geethanjali Rajan,
Commentary, Billie Dee (former Poet Laureat of the U.S.
National Library Service)

# Award Credits

"food truck," selected Golden Haiku, Golden Triangle Business Improvement District, Washington DC, Golden Haiku Poetry Contest, 2019

"paper tiger," selected Golden Haiku, Golden Triangle Business Improvement District, Washington DC, Golden Haiku Poetry Contest, 2020

"social media," Second Place, Sonic Boom Sixth Annual Senryu Contest, 2020

"the moon," Sakura Award, United States, Vancouver cherry blossom festival's haiku invitational, 2021

*The Amazing Glass House: A Haiku Storybook* by Susan Beth Furst, Honorable Mention, Children's Poetry Books and Children's Picture Books, Royal Dragonfly Book Award, 2021

"slow day," selected Golden Haiku, Golden Triangle Business Improvement District, Washington DC, Golden Haiku Poetry Contest, 2023

"in the secret garden," Nomination, Dwarf Star Award, Science fiction & Fantasy Poetry Association, 2019

"dandelions," Nomination, The Haiku Foundation Touchstone Award for individual poem, 2023

"rabbit," Nomination, Red Moon Anthology of English-Language Haiku, 2023

# Meet Susan

Through the eyes of Susan Beth, a child of the 1950s, ducks talk and mice are steamboat captains, and woodpeckers become sailors hanging out in wartime bars—flirting with cockatiel waitresses to the sound of ukulele bands.

backyard movies glitter on a silver screen

And there is music—piano lessons, violin, transistor radios, her first record player, Petula, The Beatles, Rod McKuen. Everything and everywhere is music. It's in the air. It's in her.

Old upright her fingers tickle the ivories

At the theater, the candy girl butters up the popcorn and buys the last box of Raisinets. At closing-time, she turns out the lights, locks the storage room door, and climbs the balcony steps. She smiles in the dark as

rooftop stars take a front row seat

# Author's Bio

Susan Beth Furst is an award-winning haiku poet and Children's picture book author. She is the founding editor of the Instagram Journal, *Word on the Street Haiku*, and a certified ukulele teacher and aficionado.

You can find her on Instagram.

@haikuukulele
@sueshaikus
@wordonthestreethaiku

www.literaryfurst.com

Thank you to everyone who has helped to make my first poetry collection a reality, especially Alan Summers, Christine L. Villa, and d.Perry. To all of the haiku friends and mentors I've met along the way, you are the jewels in my necklace.

Dearest Herb,

You are indeed my Prince Charming! I shall try
to be a worthy Princess.

Love,
Susan

Senior moment
She turns her prince
Into a frog

P.S. Oops!

Made in the USA
Middletown, DE
22 March 2024

51914566R00081